LUCIE RIE

This book is from a series about Modern Women Artists published by Eiderdown Books.

Other titles available from the same series:

01 *Sylvia Pankhurst*
by Katy Norris

02 *Frances Hodgkins*
by Samantha Niederman

03 *Marlow Moss*
by Lucy Howarth

04 *Laura Knight*
by Alice Strickland

05 *Lee Miller*
by Ami Bouhassane

06 *Eileen Agar*
by Laura Smith

07 *Nina Hamnett*
by Alicia Foster

08 *Eileen Mayo*
by Sara Cooper

09 *Lucie Rie*
by Isabella Smith

To order books, please visit eiderdownbooks.com

LUCIE RIE

Isabella Smith

EIDERDOWN
BOOKS

MODERN WOMEN ARTISTS

1. Lucie Rie throwing at the wheel, photographed by Jane Coper, early 1960s

'I hardly dare breathe', whispered an awe-struck David Attenborough in a 1982 BBC documentary.[1] He was not witnessing animal antics, however – the veteran broadcaster was in the London studio of Lucie Rie (1902–95), watching the greatest female potter of her generation at work.

After throwing deftly at the wheel, Rie opened her top-loading kiln to reveal a batch of newly fired vessels to the camera crew. Emptying it necessitated a lunge downwards – one that saw the diminutive 80-year old become stuck with her legs in the air. 'Dignity could hardly have survived such an episode', Attenborough later remembered.[2] And yet, somehow, it did. Dignity and elegance were defining qualities both of the woman, always dressed in white despite the muck and mess of a pottery studio, and of the work.

Across a 60-year career, Rie continually explored and evolved ceramic forms, glazes and surfaces. Her focus was always on tableware and vessels, rather than the purely sculptural. To this she brought a continental modernist sensibility that, when she first began her career in Britain, flew in the face of the studio pottery establishment. Many of her forms have achieved iconic status: her side-handled pourers and monochrome, sgraffito-decorated tableware; her vases with wide, flared rims, thrown in two parts then joined together; her bowls poised above a fine, slim foot. This aesthetic had its roots in her early life in Vienna, where she absorbed the avant-garde arts of her time – in particular, architecture – which informed the pared-back minimalism of her initial work.

After Hitler's rise to power led to her flight from Nazi-controlled Austria in 1938 – Rie was Jewish – she settled in a small mews house near Hyde Park, where she lived and worked until her death in 1995. Visitors invited to the apartment above the workshop were treated to her famously gracious hospitality, and offered homemade Sachertorte – an Austrian chocolate cake – alongside very British rock cakes. Today, Britain's role in welcoming refugees from war-torn Europe (or failing to welcome them, as the case may be) is once again of vital importance. In this context, celebrating the great cultural contribution made by this émigré potter matters more than ever.

By the end of her life, Rie had become an icon, garlanded with awards including an OBE, a CBE, a DBE and an honorary doctorate from the Royal College of Art. Yet at the time she began working in the 1920s, a woman thrower – for Rie invariably chose the wheel over hand-building – was a rarity. Women (known as 'paintresses') were far more likely to decorate wares in industrial settings than set up their own independent studios as artist–potters. Her lifetime coincided with great changes not only in Europe's political life, but in the practise and conception of ceramic art.

Early Years: Vienna

Lucie Marie Gomperz was born on 16 March 1902 to a well-off Jewish family living in the heart of Vienna. Their home, a spacious flat on 13 Elisabethstrasse, neighboured the Kunsthistorisches Museum (Art History Museum) and the Akademie der bildenden Künste (Academy of Fine Arts): a suitably cultured setting for this enlightened, liberal family. Lucie's father, Benjamin, was a doctor specialising in aural and nasal diseases, who counted Dr Sigmund Freud – the pioneering inventor of psychoanalysis – among his many distinguished clients.

Fin-de-siècle Vienna was a place of contrasts. The radical art and ideas that were bubbling up in the city's cafés and salons existed uneasily alongside the religious, cultural and political conservatism of the establishment. Emperor Franz Josef I, who had ruled much of central Europe since 1848, presided over a city that seemed unchangeable: a bastion of imperial stability and grandeur.

Lucie was raised as a sheltered child, the only daughter of three. During the summer, the family would travel to the countryside, to the luxurious home of her mother Gisela Gomperz's (née Wolf's) family in Eisenstadt, where the children – the boys clad in lederhosen – romped across the woods and fields. It was, in many respects, an idyllic childhood. As she grew older, her Uncle Sandor – Alexander Wolf – became an increasingly important figure in her life. An avid collector of art and antiquities, and a producer of both Kosher and non-Kosher wines, he indulged a passion for amateur archaeology in his vineyards.

It was here, among the vines, that Lucie first encountered sherds of finely thrown Roman red clay pots. Their elegant simplicity of form and elevated profiles, raised lightly above a narrow foot, later proved to be an inspiration for her own work. As she would recall: 'There were these fantastic Roman bowls that were floating. I always tried to copy those floating bowls.'[3] Uncle Sandor's eclectic collection, gathered on trips around the world, featured folk art, paintings and Judaica alongside archaeological artefacts. He encouraged her cultural interests, steering her away from the sciences – which also interested her – towards the arts.

When in June 1914 the archduke Franz Ferdinand, the heir to the Austrian throne, was shot in Sarajevo, the Austro-Hungarian Empire went to war. With it, the pleasure-loving Vienna of pastries and parties, waltzes and operettas, changed abruptly – as did the idyll of Lucie's childhood. Her two brothers, Paul and Teddy, soon enlisted in the army aged just 16 and 17. Like the rest of the city, the Gomperz family was affected by increased food costs and shortages, and Lucie grieved deeply when Paul was killed at the Italian Front in 1917. When war ended a year later, city-dwellers were battered by inflation and scarcity, surviving thanks to famine relief measures.

But as normality began to return, Lucie was able to finish her school education and then, in 1922, enrol in the Viennese Kunstgewerbeschule: a vocational art and craft school. She had expected to study sculpture but on her first day saw a pottery wheel and was, as she said, 'lost to it'.[4] She would focus on throwing at the wheel for the rest of her life.

A Vocation

Her formative years had coincided with an extraordinary flowering of creativity in Vienna. This spanned the Vienna Secession, a turn-of-the-century art movement that included leading artists Gustav Klimt and Egon Schiele (whose premature death in 1918 Lucie had mourned), to the Wiener Werkstätte, the co-operative association to which the Kunstgewerbeschule was closely tied. Her father Benjamin frequented the Werkstätte's showroom and had often brought the young Lucie with him, nurturing her eye for contemporary art and design.

At the Kunstgewerbeschule, she was taught by head of ceramics Michael Powolny, whose father had been a peasant potter making tiled stoves. Powolny's tastes were not in line with the progressive art movements of the day: he specialised in making porcelain figurines of cherubs. Lucie's own aesthetic was more aligned with the principles of the Werkstätte, which was founded on the belief that all design objects should be shaped by their relationship to their architectural contexts. With that in mind, her earthenware designs – all thrown – were deliberately simple and seemingly straightforward, well-suited to the elegant austerity of cutting-edge architecture. The Werkstätte school was headed by its charismatic co-founder Josef Hoffmann, an architect and designer who saw Lucie's potential: in 1923, he chose her first glazed pots for display in his masterpiece, the Palais Stoclet in Brussels. These very

2. Earthenware lobed bowl, *c.*1926

earliest pieces were colourful, featuring painterly glazes and details such as lobed rims and cut-out patterns (Fig. 2).

While studying, a growing friendship with Hans Rie, a manager at a felt-hat factory, led to a relationship. Their engagement took place largely in order to stop tongues wagging; still young, Lucie appeared not to realise the magnitude of marriage, later describing their union as 'an accident'.[5] They wed quickly, in September 1926, shortly after her graduation. It was not a happy marriage. The couple soon turned away from one another – Hans more interested in card games and sports, and Lucie retreating into her training as a potter. Her pots from this period are marked 'L.R.G. Wien': Lucie Rie Gomperz, Vienna.

With financial support from Uncle Sandor, the couple moved from the Rie family home into a rooftop flat at 24 Wollzeile, in which Rie soon had a wheel and, later, in 1933, a kiln (Fig. 3). Before the kiln's arrival, she would wrap unfired pots in newspaper, then take them by tram to be fired elsewhere – a perilous routine, given the extreme fragility of unfired clay. The apartment became a fitting setting for her work. Its interior was meticulously designed by avant-garde architect Ernst Plischke in 1928, who had even measured Hans' legs before calculating the proportions of its furniture. The environment Plischke and Rie co-created was ascetic in its clean, restrained modernist lines, and combined high-quality natural materials and craftsmanship in a neutral colour palette.

Minimal bowls and cylindrical vessels predominated her output during this period (Fig. 4). She gave them visual interest through glaze concoctions that created pitted, pockmarked or flowing, lava-like surfaces. The chemically challenging nature of such glazes was testament both to her power of invention and her interest in the sciences. Alongside these one-off pieces, she specialised in tea sets of burnished red terracotta. These unglazed pieces rely on modernist silhouettes, immaculately curving handles and a buffed finish for their visual appeal. The early influence of those Roman bowls is apparent in their

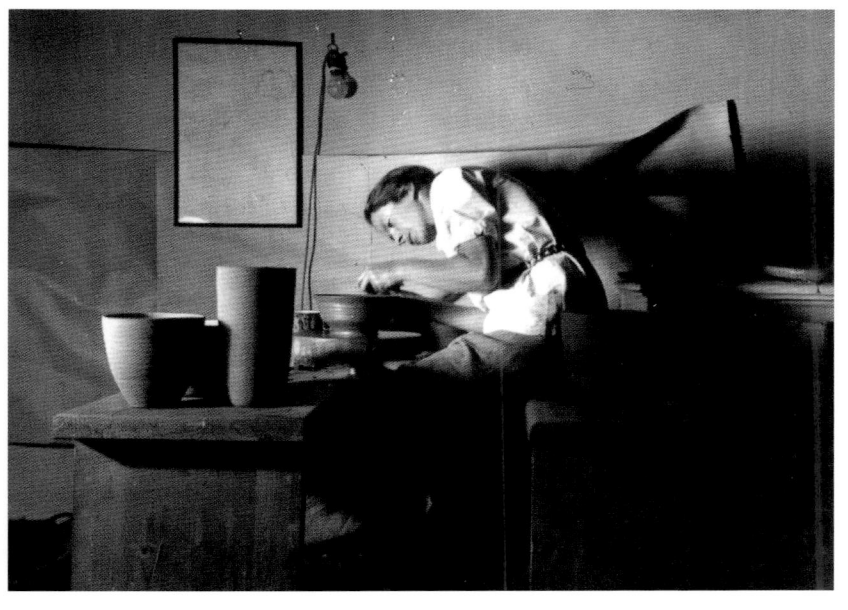

3. Lucie Rie working in her home studio in Vienna, 1930

4. Earthenware vases with layered glazes, c.1930

5. Unglazed earthenware tea set with a burnished finish, *c*.1936

6. (above) Unglazed speckled earthenware bowl and saucer, *c.*1936
7. (below) Glazed earthenware tea set, *c.*1930

undecorated simplicity and strength of form (Figs 5 and 6). Once Rie had her own kiln, she began to raw-glaze her pots. This meant that instead of glazing pieces that had already been fired once at a low temperature (known as bisque-firing), she glazed raw, unfired pots – a risky technique, but one she soon mastered. Eliminating a firing from the process, she discovered, was both economical and created richer surfaces.

Before long, Rie's focus on potting paid off, with work shown at the Lobmeyr gallery, the Bimini gallery and the Werkbund. Her work was not universally appreciated, however. Attempts at selling through the Werkstätte led to not a single sale, perhaps because her style did not pander to a fashion for folk art-inspired pottery. Though architects responded to her work, fellow craftspeople thought its simplicity unsophisticated (Fig. 7). Later, she recalled how Werkstätte potters such as Vally Wieselthier and Gudrun Baudisch 'tried to subdue me ... and said not very nice things about me.'[6] But further afield, she enjoyed a growing reputation: over the next decade, her pots would win gold medals at competitions in Brussels and Milan.

In 1937, Josef Hoffmann took 70 of Rie's pieces to the Paris International Exhibition. Here, in the Austrian Pavilion Hoffmann had designed, they were displayed in a purpose-built corridor of glass, and won her the second prize; the judges deemed them too repetitive to merit the first. Though her personal life was lacking – alongside an empty marriage, she also suffered a string of bereavements in the 1930s, including both parents – her professional life went from strength to strength.

War: From Vienna to London

Only a year after her successes in Paris, Rie's life was transformed. Though the Gomperzes were Jewish, they were secular; unlike the Wolf family, they didn't keep kosher and avoided trips to the synagogue with their devout relatives. But the rising tide of antisemitism left all Jews vulnerable, with a growing number of the Viennese agreeing with the far-right policies appearing in neighbouring Germany. Previously, Austrian Jews had had equality under the law (though not always borne out in practice). It was not uncommon for Vienna's Jewish families to think of themselves as Austrian first, Jewish second. Nevertheless, there lingered a sense of otherness that led to discrimination – a discrimination that became dramatically worse following Adolf Hitler's rise to power in Germany in 1933 and the growth of the right wing in Austria.

Some of Rie's former friends hung Nazi flags from their windows; social invitations from non-Jewish friends dried up. The man who assisted her with kiln firings wore a Nazi armband, and the Wiener Werkstätte split into Aryan and Jewish membership groups. Rie was deeply shocked by the rapid transformation in attitudes: a trauma that left her slow to trust for the rest of her life. In March 1938, the Anschluss – the annexation of Austria for the German Empire – took place. She later recalled lying awake the night it happened, sleepless from the noise of 'Sieg heil' ('Hail victory') shouted by crowds in the street.

It became clear that the Rie-Gomperzes, like so many others, were no longer safe. The Nazis had taken over the family house in Eisenstadt and Uncle Sandor had been imprisoned. The couple pulled every string possible to gain the documents that would enable them to flee to England, travelling to London as refugees in October 1938. In her application to move to Britain, Rie described herself as 'working only at original pottery in plain shapes and delicate shades. I was kept very busy and my orders increased continually. My customers were private people, architects and shops in Vienna as well as abroad.'[7]

The Ries found a flat in Hampstead, which had become home to many others who had escaped Vienna. Friends in the same situation included Freud's architect son, Ernst Freud, and the artist Fritz Lampl, whose glass-blowing workshop and gallery, Bimini – which had exhibited Lucie's pots – he re-established in London.

As her husband focused on supporting fellow refugees, and Rie helped cook and care for new arrivals, she also turned her attention towards learning about the British studio pottery scene and searching for a workshop for hire. Though undoubtedly a deeply challenging period, she also experienced excitement: escape from Vienna also held all the possibilities of a new beginning. Soon, the pair parted in an amicable separation. Hans left for the United States in 1939, leaving Rie alone in London. After the marriage was dissolved, her potter's mark changed to either 'RIE' or 'LR' – the disappearance of 'Gomperz' also rendering her name less alien-sounding, at a time when the British public were deeply suspicious of foreigners.

Rie took to walking the streets in search of a studio with accommodation. Finding herself in a mews on the north side of Hyde Park – at that time a run-down backwater – she spotted a garage with a small, one-bed flat above. She would live and work at 18 Albion Mews for the rest of her life. War broke out as she moved in; one of her first tasks was to install black-out curtains. Plischke's bespoke furniture was shipped from Vienna at great expense and adapted for the modest space by her friend Ernst Freud. This furniture would go on to provide a tie to the past, connecting to the idea current in Vienna's art world of the 'Gesamtkunstwerk' – the total work of art that comprised every element in a given space. For the rest of her life, Plischke's walnut-wood cupboards, chairs, fitted storage and tables would frame and contextualise Rie's work (Fig. 8). (Today, the set is in the permanent collection of the Möbelmuseum Wien in Vienna.)

8. (overleaf) Lucie Rie's display area in her Albion Mews flat c. 1970s, featuring furniture by Ernst Plischke

The Button Factory

From early 1941, 'war work' was made compulsory for women aged 18 to 60 – mandatory labour, often in professional fields previously closed to their sex. Rie's job was adjusting optical instruments and spectrographs at a lens factory: work that was poorly paid and tedious. To supplement her income, her friend, lover and fellow refugee Fritz Lampl invited her to work from 5am until 7.30am at Orplid, his glass workshop (previously known as Bimini). She returned for a few hours each evening after her shift – while also working as an air-raid warden. Here they made glass buttons based on antique seals and coins from the British Museum, meeting the need for buttons that had arisen as factories focused their production on uniforms.

Though rationing meant strict rules around the range and availability of clothes, buttons – and other small luxuries such as make-up – were deemed necessary for public morale. After writing many letters asking to be released from war work, Rie was finally permitted to focus on button-making full-time. When Lampl's Soho workshop was bombed, Rie began making ceramic buttons in her own small studio instead. As German bombers made relentless attacks on the capital, she sheltered in the crypt of a chapel nearby; her home survived with only minor damage.

She hand-formed or threw each button, using these to create moulds from which multiples could be made rapidly. Some were plain, round buttons, versatile and tasteful; others were lavishly sculpted and glazed in a rainbow of hues (Figs 9 and 10). Designs bore names such as 'Lettuce', 'Stars' or 'Primrose Edith'. Rie also made other small ceramic accessories: umbrella handles, buckles and a few pieces of jewellery.

The buttons proved popular. As orders increased, Rie employed other Jewish refugees to assist in what became known as 'the Button Factory in Albion Mews', coming to Rie through William Ohly, owner of the Berkeley Gallery in Mayfair. At its peak, she

9. (above) Glazed ceramic buttons, c.1940–45 **10.** (overleaf) Glazed ceramic buttons on a sample board used by a travelling salesman, bearing labels to identify each design, c.1940–45

employed 18 people who produced over 6,000 buttons a month. She received orders from fashion houses such as Worth and Jacqmar, and leading couturiers such as Victor Stiebel would visit with swatches of cloth, asking her to create buttons matching their precise hue.

Though her own appreciation of fine fabrics made it a not unpleasant enterprise, the strains of the war and of loneliness made it a challenging period. One assistant, Monika Kinley, later recalled: 'She was then in her mid-forties, her success on the continent lay behind her and seemed to carry no weight in this country. To me she appeared to be a sad and worried woman, very much on her own.'[8] However, colour-matching buttons led to a deep knowledge of glaze compositions – Rie became able to create a perfectly matched button within only a day or two.

Rie and Coper: 'cabbage days'

Between making up orders of buttons, Rie would quietly throw pots on the wheel. Her throwing technique was fastidiously tidy, free of splashing and mess. She had been taught to throw using a minimal amount of water, wetting her fingertips just enough to prevent them sticking to the surface of the pot: unlike British potters, she used no tray to catch excess water or clay.

Rie used two continental kick-wheels: electricity-free devices reliant on the potter kicking a heavy flywheel at its base, creating enough momentum to throw pots. The wheels were installed in front of windows overlooking the tangled greenery of an old cemetery, to make use of the natural light. There was a pair of old-fashioned scales, shipped from Vienna along with her electric kiln; shelves were installed above a small stove, where pots could dry. Button moulds were stacked high to the ceiling.

Rie had arrived in London with only a suitcaseful of pots, many of which cracked in transit. Not long after her arrival, she took her precious remaining pieces to a meeting with Bernard Leach, then the leading figure and spokesperson of the British studio pottery movement, seeking advice on beginning her career in England. The older potter was damning in his verdict of her earthenware pieces, describing them as 'too thickly glazed, thinly potted, too much like stoneware [...] with no humanity.'[9] Her meeting with the other great ceramicist of the day, William Staite Murray, head of pottery at the Royal College of Art, was no better. She visited hoping for a signature that would allow her a work permit. She gained the signature, but he refused her handshake. It was clear that the reputation she had gained on the continent counted for little in England. Meetings with the keeper of ceramics at the Victoria and Albert Museum (V&A) and London's leading craft gallerists saw her work met, again, with a complete lack of comprehension. They were deeply discouraging experiences.

Leach and Rie had met in 1939 at Shinner's Bridge Pottery, part of a utopian community based at Dartington Hall in Devon. Leach was focused on his notion of the 'right' way of making, based on an Eastern aesthetic – he had studied ceramics in Japan – blended with England's country pottery traditions. The result: an idiosyncratic mix of East and West, for which he became a remarkable evangelist. Rie tried briefly to incorporate his style – which by that point was British studio pottery's dominant style – into her own work, even meekly attending his course for beginners despite her years of experience. The results were not inspired. Nevertheless, Leach soon became a close friend. After their first meeting, she wrote to him saying: 'I want to thank you again. [...] You did remind me that there is something else besides Hitler and refugee's problems and the need to earn money ... I had forgotten it.'[10]

Back in London, with the Button Factory in action and Rie's potting largely put to one side, the arrival of a new assistant – another Jewish refugee – would prove to be momentous. Hans Coper was born in Germany in 1920; much of his life had been

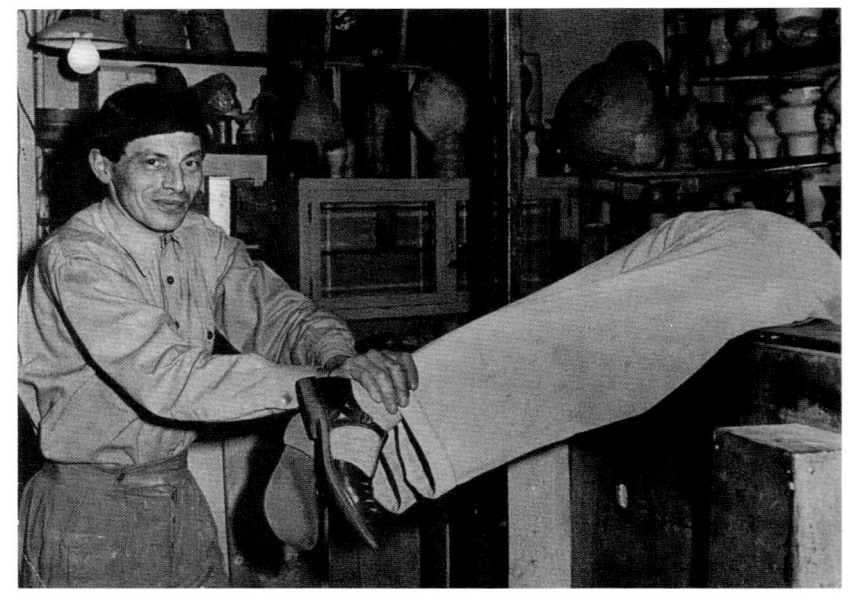

11. Hans Coper holding Lucie Rie's legs while she unpacks the top-loading kiln at Albion Mews, *c.*1950

spent on the move, hounded by the Gestapo. He had endured periods in an internment camp and hard labour in conditions so poor they had provoked a physical breakdown. By the end of the war in 1945, Coper was working at a factory and painting in his spare time. When in 1946 William Ohly met Coper through London's refugee network, he suggested that Coper ask Rie for work. Coper had never previously touched clay, but proved so adept at button-making that Rie arranged for him to study throwing. He returned proficient after just one week's tuition: no small feat.

The working relationship blossomed and, perhaps surprisingly, she would later state that 'he knew much more than I did.'[11] This was despite their age gap – she was 44, he was 26 – and potting being entirely new to him. What had begun as a working relationship soon became a deeply committed friendship (Fig. 11). When Rie showed him her Viennese pots alongside those in a quasi-Leachean style, he was emphatic that the early pieces were far better; the latter did not give voice to her personal talents. It was precisely the encouragement that Rie needed, at precisely the moment she needed it most. What Coper gave Rie was a bolstered sense of cultural identity in the face of the British artistic establishment: a confidence in her own aesthetic vision, which no British potter had been willing to give her.

Bread and Butter: Turning Towards Tableware

Two years after the war ended, factories ceased war work and soon restarted normal production. This meant there was no longer a demand for hand-made buttons, and by 1947, Rie was at last able to focus on pottery. The button-makers all left, bar Coper and an assistant. Coper stayed not as an apprentice or an assistant – Rie was firm on this point – but as an equal. It was a partnership that would last for the next decade.

Though industrial potteries had been allowed to resume full production after the war's end, the government forbade sales of decorated pieces to the domestic market. With all ornamented wares reserved for export, only white, undecorated 'Utility' tableware could be sold at home – a policy that stayed in place until the early 1950s. The public's desire for more attractive products led to a swift upswing in demand for handmade ceramics. It was a headwind that helped the two potters weather the difficult post-war years.

Together they made tableware: tea sets, breakfast sets and serving bowls became their bread and butter (Fig. 12). Rie soon moved from earthenware to stoneware, ordering a huge, expensive kiln capable of firing to the necessary high temperatures. Rie avoided leaving the throwing rings – concentric fingermarks made while pulling up the walls of a piece – that were a totem of the Leachean style. Instead, she trimmed pots before smoothing them with an old-fashioned safety razor blade. Despite the fineness of her thin-walled works, Rie continued to raw-glaze: a technical feat that, in less capable hands, would result in pots collapsing from the glaze's moisture. A limited colour palette allowed the potters to standardise and maximise their output. An opaque tin-based white glaze coated inner areas, which were enlivened by speckles and pinholes – usually considered a flaw, transformed here into a stylistic feature – while a matte chocolate brown of manganese oxide mixed with gum arabic coated exterior surfaces (Fig. 13).

During a trip to Salisbury Plain, Rie saw Bronze Age pots in an Avebury museum that had been decoratively incised using bird bones. This inspired her use of sgraffito (in Italian, 'scratched'): a technique of scraping through a layer of glaze to create patterns the colour of the clay hidden beneath (Fig. 14). She used a pin or needle to create simple, sketch-like designs of lines and bands. One key innovation was in pulling bowls to one side to create an asymmetrical pouring lip: a design both simple, practical and modern (Fig. 15).

Unlike the 'standard ware' being produced at the Leach Pottery in St Ives, which was heavy, rustic and came freighted

12. Stoneware tea cup and saucer with manganese glaze and sgraffito, impressed with both Lucie Rie and Hans Coper's marks, 1950s

13. Stoneware side-handled coffee pot with manganese glaze and sgraffito decoration, c.1965

14. Necklace of press-moulded porcelain beads with manganese glaze and sgraffito design, strung on a black ribbon, mid-1950s

15. Stoneware bowl with white glaze, manganese rim and integrated manganese speckle, *c.*1956

16. Porcelain covered bowl with inlay on exterior and sgraffito on interior manganese glaze on the interior, lip and handle, *c.*1958

with philosophical ideas around hand-making, these wares – informed by European modernism, owing almost nothing to tradition – were light and elegant, driven by aesthetics, not ideals. Rie had never been inclined to philosophise about her work. Her sole concession to intellectualising came in her short *Credo* of 1950: 'If one should ask me whether I believe myself to be a modern potter or a potter of tradition, I would answer I don't know and I don't care.' She added: 'Art theories have no meaning for me; beauty has. This is all my philosophy.'[12]

The pots were not designed to be cheap, and soon became prized in the most urbane of settings and a firm favourite on wedding gift lists (Fig. 16). Leach introduced Rie to the Heal's team, who soon became buyers, as did Liberty and the Bendick's café chain. In these early days there was little time to experiment with one-off works. She later called this period of hard graft the 'cabbage days': cabbage for lunch and dinner.[13]

A Metropolitan Potter

Rie's investment in the high-firing electric kiln opened the door to greater experimentation. She was keen to try glazes from Leach's seminal *A Potter's Book* (1940), but as she was unable to reach the 1300°C necessary to create his stoneware glazes, she improvised, modifying recipes so they would vitrify – melt and become glass-like – at 1260°C. One favourite was a mirror-like black glaze, which she had tweaked to become silkier and more lustrous. From 1949, she also experimented with porcelain. Leach had previously criticised her electric-fired work as being 'dead', due to the lack of flame.[14] Live-flame kilns fired with wood, gas, coal or oil, which created hazy atmospheres that encouraged variable surface effects, and were deemed far superior. Compared to these, electric kilns were more like a white-hot domestic oven: clean and clear-firing.

By adapting Leach's glazes for an electric kiln, Rie was staking a claim for the urban potter, at a time when Leach was

17. Pots by Lucie Rie and Hans Coper on the workshop shelves in Albion Mews, 1950s

preaching about the potter's place in country life. A kiln with open flames would have been deeply impractical in her tiny central London home, without outdoor space and with anti-smog regulations in force. What she achieved in her city studio was a balance between the excitement of metropolitan life, with all its bustle and sophistication, with the peace of what was then seen as a rural profession.

While Rie and Coper made tableware stamped with both of their potter's marks, as time passed they also created an increasing number of individual works (Fig. 17). Coper made larger, monochrome sculptural pieces with dry, matte surfaces, while Rie broadened and refined a range of forms, motifs and glazes, exploring illustrative ornamentation reminiscent of textile designs and bolder, more textural finishes (Fig. 18).

As the new decade began, Rie started to exhibit work in spaces such as the Berkeley Gallery and Henry Rothschild's Primavera Gallery. In 1951, the potters were featured in the Festival of Britain: a national exhibition designed 'to show what the modern world owes to British achievements', celebrating contemporary art and design, science, technology and architecture.[15] Eight and a half million people visited the South Bank exhibition – its principal attraction – which included work by the two refugees. That year, Rie also represented Britain at the Milan Triennale, and was rewarded with a gold medal for her efforts.

When *The New York Times* interviewed Rie following a successful outing to the United States, she said of her future plans: 'I hope to keep my workroom small, but I would like a factory to turn out some of my cups and saucers.' (Fig. 19)[16] In 1960, Wedgwood invited Rie to create prototypes for tea and coffee sets in their traditional blue and white Jasperware clays. Rie presented the directors with four cup designs, the blue body ornamented with bands of inlaid white. They declined to take the commission further; stung, it was to be her only dalliance with industry.

18. Planter made of stoneware clay mixed with manganese with an off-white glaze and applied panels, c.1965

19. Stoneware breakfast service, white glaze with manganese rims, commissioned by the printmaker Robin Tanner, 1958–60

The Albion Mews studio had always been tight for space, but as the pair's work gained in stature, sharing the workshop became increasingly impractical. In 1958, Coper moved to Hertfordshire to establish a studio where he could make large pieces. Over the next decade, Rie's profile grew and grew: her work was exhibited as far afield as Holland, Japan, Australia and Germany, despite her misgivings. Austria was a step too far, however: 'You can do it when I'm dead.'[17]

Teapots – For Discipline

It was at 64 years old, after almost 40 years of potting, that an exhibition came about which consolidated Rie's position at the forefront of her field. The Arts Council's *Lucie Rie: A retrospective exhibition of earthenware, stoneware and porcelain 1926–1967* at its London premises comprised a mammoth 300 works. One new development was on show: vases made from differently coloured clays incompletely mixed together which, when thrown, created dramatic swirls flowing upwards; body and decoration are one (Fig. 20). Although this was not a new technique – the eighteenth-century potter Francis Place used the same process – Rie made it entirely her own.

In the catalogue, exhibition organiser and V&A curator George Wingfield Digby wrote: 'Here was a studio potter whose work was not rustic but metropolitan.'[18] Recanting his earlier opinion of her work, Leach commented: 'An outstanding quality of Lucie's work is the degree to which it is free from the direct influence of other potters, ancient and modern';[19] he could not have failed to notice his lack of impact on her mature practice (Fig. 21). The only person whose opinion held real sway over her output was Coper, who Rie always maintained was far greater than she. She later stated: 'I was a potter, but he was an artist.'[20]

One source of inspiration came from her own early work. In the 1970s and 1980s, she returned to her frothing glaze

20. Flared lip vase of stoneware mixed clays with an integral dolomite and cream spiral, c.1972

21. Flared lip porcelain vase with manganese glaze and terracotta-red banding with blue inlay and radiating sgraffito, *c.*1980–81

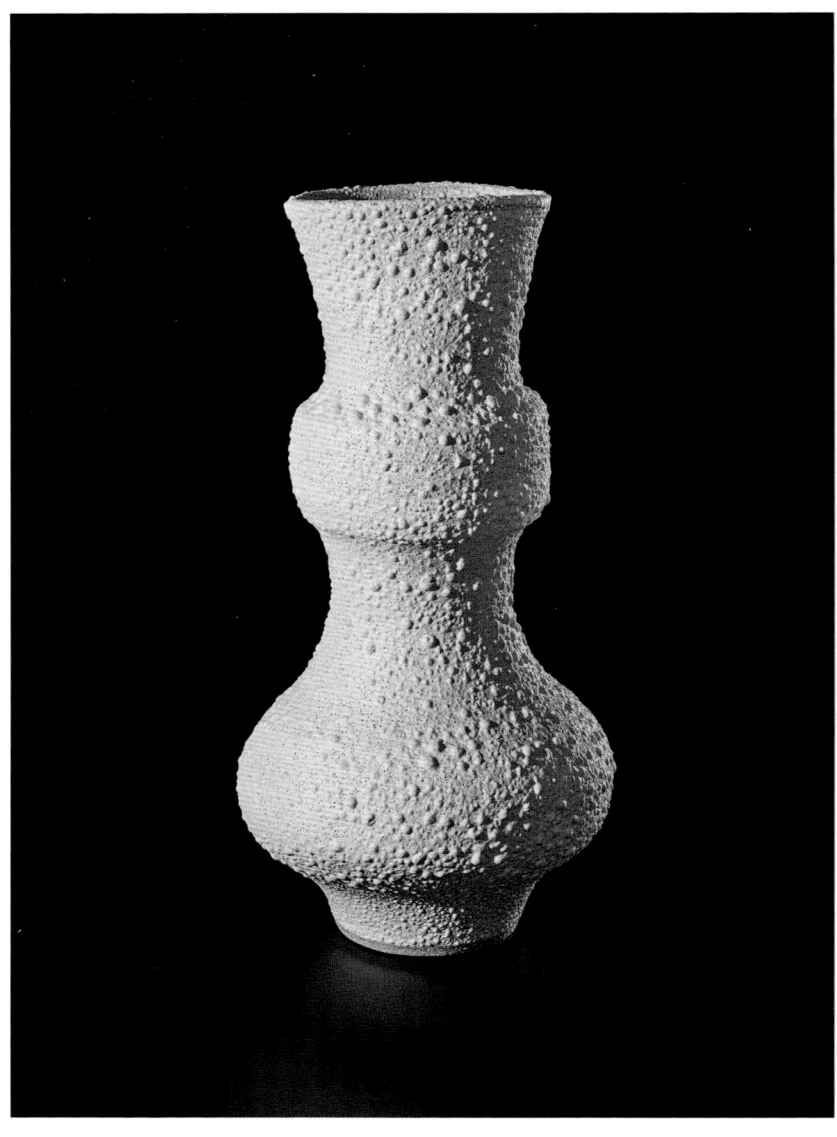

22. Large stoneware vase with pure white blistered glaze, c.1984

23. Large conical stoneware bowl, pitted and flowing cream glaze, c.1976

experiments of 50 years prior. By adding three per cent of silicon carbide to a glaze recipe, she could make dramatically textured and pitted effects (Fig. 22).

Over the years, the house in Albion Mews became a magnet for collectors and friends. Rie's hospitality was renowned: visitors invited upstairs were served tea and homemade cakes. For Bernard Leach's seventieth birthday, Rie baked a cake with icing as textured as one of her lava-like glazes (Fig. 23). Her friend Janet Leach described how Rie effortlessly straddled the artistic and the domestic: 'I have sat talking by her wheel while she makes pots, with a cake baking in the oven upstairs [...] to do three things at once, and well, is a gift.'[21]

A skill that came less naturally was teaching. Rie taught part-time at Camberwell College of Arts from 1960 to 1972, yet it was the independence of living and working alone that suited her best. Nevertheless, she felt a strong sense of duty to her pupils; Coper described her teaching style as 'like a steel hand in a velvet glove.'[22] Her illustrious students included Ian Godfrey, Ewen Henderson, Mo Jupp, John Ward and Deirdre Burnett, a list that is characterised by its stylistic variety. Rie was not interested in creating acolytes. Instead, she focused on giving students the practical skills to succeed, instructing them to make 'teapots – for discipline'.[23]

Maturity: 'prose objects' and 'poetic objects'

By the 1980s, no longer guided by economic considerations, Rie focused largely on bowls and vases, relishing their relative lack of design constraints. She was at the peak of her career: in 1987, her work was even chosen to illustrate a Royal Mail stamp, which depicted a flare-rimmed vase with pink and green-pigmented clays spiralling upwards. From early on, Rie had filled school exercise books with detailed notes on shapes, clays and glazes in a personal shorthand of marks. Her work from this time makes use of the full range of colours and finishes she had mastered across her lifetime, including the vibrant oxidised stoneware glazes she had developed for the electric kiln – from vivid turquoise to canary yellow, bright pinks to limpid bottle greens (Figs 24, 25 and the cover of this book). Bowls bear finely thrown rims coated in a metallic brown manganese oxide that drips, sometimes pooling inside.

Elsewhere, manganese oxide served as an inlay: brushed into scratched designs, sponged off then over-glazed, the inverse of her sgraffito technique. In some pieces, these lines criss-cross so closely as to create a dense, textile-like mesh, the resulting works being known as her 'knitted' pots (Fig. 26).

In 1981, Rie opened a kiln-full of work that had been coated in a white glaze. She was horrified to find the load was entirely, mysteriously, black (Fig. 27). Though not generally superstitious, she read it as a bad omen – Coper had long been in ill health – and rushed to his side. He died several days later. An undated note in Rie's handwriting reads: 'LR is indebted to HC for his guidence [sic] as a mentor & for his positive criticism & ethical spirit throughout their lifelong friendship. He gave her security & courage & her pots would not be the same without his constant help and advise [sic].'[24]

That year, the ceramic artist Alison Britton summarised what gave Rie's pots their power, writing that they are both 'prose objects' and 'poetic objects', which she characterised as: 'Those that are mainly active and those that are mainly contemplative. To me the most moving things are the ones where I experience a frisson from both these aspects at once, from both prose and poetry, purpose and commentary. These have what I call a "double presence."'[25] Though their cost put them out of the realm most consider reasonable for objects of daily use, it is this balance between beauty and function that made Rie's pieces remarkable (Fig. 28).

When the Japanese fashion designer Issey Miyake met Rie in 1984, he was so enchanted by her work that his 1989 Autumn/Winter collection included pieces adorned with her buttons.

24. Porcelain footed bowl, green glaze with manganese rim, c.1980

25. Porcelain footed bowl, yellow glaze with manganese rim, 1983

26. (above and opposite) Large stoneware bowl with 'knitted' inlaid design of manganese beneath a grey glaze, c.1978

27. Stoneware fluted bowl and bottle vase with combed design, over-fired black glaze, both from the 'black firing' of 1981

28. Porcelain footed bowl, manganese glaze with sgraffito design and blue-glazed well, *c.*1970

29. Lucie Rie at home in Albion Mews in the late 1960s, surrounded by her own and Hans Coper's pots

The same year, the exhibition *Issey Miyake meets Lucie Rie* took place at Tokyo's Sogetsu Gallery. Under Miyake's direction, pots were placed on islands on a reflective pool of water designed by the architect Tadao Ando. The graceful serenity of this set piece matched that of the potter, who was invariably clad in white. Leach was fond of saying: 'The pot is the man: his virtues and his vices are shown therein – no disguise is possible.'[26] The connection between the woman and the work, in all its cosmopolitan elegance, is clear (Fig. 29). In 1989, Miyake wrote: 'Lucie Rie's work is an accurate self-portrait of her own character; her soul is contained within these vessels.' He added:'Lucie's work embodies a world view that is unique to Western culture and history. They are also very modest, very human, and most of all, humane.'[27]

By 1990, despite her advancing age, Rie maintained a fearsome work routine that began at 5.30am and ended in the early evening. 'What else should I do?', she said. 'I am a potter.'[28] That year came the first of several strokes that left her unable to work. She died in 1995 at the age of 93. Since then, her legacy has continued to grow, inspiring new generations of potters and artists and reaching soaring results at auction. Unlike most potters, whose admirers are limited to a niche core of ceramics aficionados, Rie's status as someone slightly apart from the craft world (she refused to join any medium-specific membership organisations, for example) has meant she was never entirely siloed within her discipline, which perhaps helped her avoid posthumous obscurity. Nevertheless, her position as a potter – something she insisted upon, resisting the title of 'artist'[29] – has arguably led to far less name-recognition among the general public than a painter or sculptor of comparable standing would enjoy. Her prominent collectors have included the fashion designer Jonathan Anderson, the minimalist artist Dan Flavin – who in 1990 made a series of neon sculptures named *Untitled (to Lucie Rie, master potter)* – and, of course, the naturalist David Attenborough.

Notes

1. David Attenborough, quoted in *Omnibus*, BBC Television, 14 Feb 1982, directed by Jonathan Fulford and Cyril Frankel
2. David Attenborough, quoted in 'Lucie Rie 1902–1995', *Ceramic Review*, (Jul/Aug 1995), no. 154, p.10
3. David Sexton, 'Floating towards freedom', *The Sunday Telegraph*, 1 May 1988
4. Tony Birks, *Lucie Rie* (Catrine 1987, this edition 2017), p.20
5. Emmanuel Cooper, *Lucie Rie: Modernist Potter* (New Haven and London 2012), p.123
6. Lucie Rie, quoted in *Omnibus* (cited note 1)
7. Cooper (cited note 5), p.76
8. Emmanuel Cooper, 'Lucie Rie', *Ceramic Review* (Mar/Apr 1992), no. 134, p.26
9. Cooper (cited note 5), p.119
10. Ibid., p.122
11. Cyril Frankel, *Modern Pots: Hans Coper, Lucie Rie & their Contemporaries, The Lisa Sainsbury Collection* (London and Norwich 2000), p.16
12. Ibid., p.67
13. Ibid., p.18
14. Cooper (cited note 5), p.119
15. Sequoia Miller, 'British studio pottery in popular culture', *Things of Beauty Growing: British Studio Pottery* (New Haven, Cambridge and London 2017), p.122
16. Frankel (cited note 11), p.77
17. Ibid., p.85
18. John Houston (ed.), *Lucie Rie: A survey of her life and work* (London 1981), p.6
19. Tarby Davenport, 'Lucie Rie – A potter of our time', *Ceramic Review* (May/Jun 1974), no. 27, p.4
20. Lucie Rie quoted in 'Hands on the Wheel of Fate', *The Guardian*, 31 Aug 1988
21. Janet Leach, 'Contributions', in Houston (cited note 18), p.31
22. John Windsor, 'A slender vessel made from clay', *The Independent*, 22 Oct 1994
23. Tony Birks, 'Lucie Rie, Hans Coper and their Teaching', *Lucie Rie, Hans Coper and Their Pupils* (Norwich 1990), p.11

24 Undated, unsigned note in Lucie Rie's handwriting in the Crafts Study Centre archive (reference code: 2002.26.57 Rie/4/5)
25 Alison Britton, 'Essays', *The Maker's Eye* (London 1981), p.16
26 Bernard Leach, *The Potter's Challenge* (New York 1975), p.48
27 Fax from Miyake Design Studio dated 4 Jun 1989 in the Crafts Study Centre archive (reference code: RIE 11/12/1)
28 Frankel (cited note 11), p.80
29 See footnote 20

Image credits

Cover. Porcelain footed bowl with pink inlaid radiating lines, turquoise and manganese bands, *c.*1978. Photograph: © Phillips Auctioneers Limited.

1. Lucie Rie throwing at the wheel, early 1960s. Photo by Jane Coper © Jane Coper / Estate of the artist.
2. Lobed bowl, earthenware, *c.*1926, given to the Victoria and Albert Museum by Lucie Rie. Photo: © Victoria and Albert Museum, London.
3. Lucie Rie working in her home studio in Vienna, 1930. From the Crafts Study Centre, University for the Creative Arts, 2005.40. © Estate of Lucie Rie.
4. Earthenware vases with layered glazes, *c.*1930. Photo: © Byron Slater Photography, courtesy of Phillips Auctioneers Ltd.
5. Unglazed earthenware tea set with a burnished finish, *c.*1936. Photo: © Victoria and Albert Museum, London.
6. Unglazed speckled earthenware bowl and saucer, *c.*1936. Photo: © Byron Slater Photography, courtesy of Phillips Auctioneers Ltd.
7. Glazed earthenware tea set, *c.*1930. Photo: Michael Harvey, courtesy of Erskine, Hall & Coe.
8. Lucie Rie's display area in her Albion Mews flat, featuring furniture by Ernst Plischke. From the Crafts Study Centre, University for the Creative Arts, RIE/20/5/2/14. © Estate of Lucie Rie. *c.*1970s.
9. Glazed ceramic buttons on a sample board used by a travelling salesman, bearing labels to identify each design, *c.*1940–45. Photo: Takao Ohya, courtesy of a private collection, Japan.
10. Glazed ceramic buttons, *c.*1940–45. Photo: Takao Ohya, courtesy of a private collection, Japan.
11. Hans Coper holding Lucie Rie's legs while she unpacks the top-loading kiln at Albion Mews, *c.*1950. Photo by Stella Snead. From the Crafts Study Centre, University for the Creative Arts, 2005.40. © Estate of Lucie Rie.
12. Stoneware tea cup and saucer with manganese glaze and sgraffito, *c.*1950s. Photo: courtesy of Sotheby's, private collection.
13. Stoneware side-handled coffee pot with manganese glaze and sgraffito decoration, *c.*1965. Photo: © Byron Slater Photography, courtesy estate of the artist.

14. Necklace of press-moulded porcelain beads with manganese glaze and sgraffito design, strung on a black ribbon, mid-1950s. From the Crafts Study Centre, University for the Creative Arts, P.91.1. © Estate of Lucie Rie / Crafts Study Centre.
15. Stoneware bowl with white glaze, manganese rim and integrated manganese speckle, c.1956. Photo: © Phillips Auctioneers Ltd.
16. Porcelain covered bowl with inlay on exterior and sgraffito on interior, manganese glaze on the interior, lip and handle, c.1958. Photo: Phillips Auctioneers Ltd.
17. Pots by Lucie Rie and Hans Coper on the workshop shelves in Albion Mews, 1950s. Photo by Jane Coper © Estates of the artists.
18. Planter made of stoneware clay mixed with manganese with an off-white glaze and applied panels, c.1965. Photo: © Byron Slater Photography, courtesy of Phillips Auctioneers Ltd.
19. Stoneware breakfast service, white glaze with manganese rims, commissioned by the printmaker Robin Tanner, 1958–60. From the Crafts Study Centre, University for the Creative Arts, P.91.2. © Estate of Lucie Rie / Crafts Study Centre.
20. Flared lip vase of stoneware mixed clays with an integral dolomite and cream spiral, c.1972. Photo: © Phillips Auctioneers Ltd.
21. Flared lip porcelain vase with manganese glaze and terracotta-red banding with blue inlaid and radiating sgraffito, c.1980–81. Photo: courtesy of Christie's Images. From the Collection of the late Victoria, Lady de Rothschild.
22. Large stoneware vase with pure white blistered glaze, c.1984. Photo: © Byron Slater Photography, courtesy of Phillips Auctioneers Limited.
23. Large conical stoneware bowl, pitted and flowing cream glaze, c.1976. Photo: © Byron Slater Photography, courtesy of Phillips Auctioneers Ltc.
24. Porcelain footed bowl, green glaze with manganese rim, c.1980. Photo: © Byron Slater Photography, courtesy of Phillips Auctioneers Ltd.
25. Porcelain footed bowl, yellow glaze with manganese rim, 1983. Photo: © Phillips Auctioneers Ltd.
26. Large stoneware bowl with 'knitted' inlaid design of manganese beneath a grey glaze, c.1978. Photo: © Byron Slater Photography, courtesy of Phillips Auctioneers Ltd.
27. Stoneware fluted bowl and bottle vase with combed design, over-fired black glaze, both from the 'black firing' of 1981. Photo: © Byron Slater Photography, courtesy of Phillips Auctioneers Ltd.
28. Porcelain footed bowl, manganese glaze with sgraffito design and blue-glazed well, c.1970. Photo: © Byron Slater Photography, courtesy of Phillips Auctioneers Ltd.
29. Lucie Rie at home in Albion Mews in the late 1960s, surrounded by her own and Hans Coper's pots. Photo by Jane Coper © Estates of the artists.

About the author

Isabella Smith has been immersed in ceramic art since 2014, when she began working as a research assistant for a private collector of British studio pottery. After an art history MA at the Courtauld Institute, which focused on the use of clay in performance art, she worked as an editor – first at *Ceramic Review* magazine and then at the Crafts Council's magazine, *Crafts*. She is currently senior editor at *Apollo* and has contributed to publications including *ArtReview*, *Frieze*, the *Guardian* and *The TLS*. *Lucie Rie* published by Eiderdown Books is her first book.

Acknowledgements

Thank you to Harriet Olsen, founder of Eiderdown Books, for including Lucie Rie in her excellent Modern Women Artists series, and to Ben Williams for his invaluable help as a representative of the artist's estate. I'm grateful for support from staff at the Crafts Study Centre (CSC) at the University for the Creative Arts in Farnham, which holds Rie's archive: Greta Bertram, Simon Olding and Shirley Dixon. A 'Ceramic Art Grant' from the Craft Pottery Charitable Trust (CPCT) funded many image licenses and my visit to the CSC archive, while an 'Image Licence Grant' from the Women's History Network (WHN) covered the remaining illustration costs. My thanks to the CPCT's trustees and the WHN team for their belief in this project and for their generosity. I must also thank the galleries, museums, auction houses and photographers who allowed us to include their images, and I acknowledge, too, all those whose writings on Rie informed my own (most importantly, Emmanuel Cooper, whose insightful biography delves deep into her Vienna years). Thank you to Daryl Fromm, who first showed me just how fascinating ceramics can be, and to my grandfather Joseph Milewski, whose stories of life as a refugee fleeing a Nazi invasion – like Rie – I will always remember.

Index

Page numbers in *italics* refer to illustrations.

18 Albion Mews 2, 13, *14–15*, *22*, *31*, 32, 35, 40

A
Anschluss 12
antisemitism in Austria 11–12
archaeological influences 3, 24
art world response to works 11, 21, 35, 41, 49
artistic influences 1–2, 3, 30
  see also archaeological influences
Arts Council exhibition 35
asymmetric designs 24, *28*
Attenborough, David 1, 49

B
Baudisch, Gudrun 11
Bendick's café chain 30
Berkeley Gallery 32
Bimini gallery 11, 12–13, 16
'black firing' 41, *46*
bowls *31*, *48*
  asymmetry 24, *28*
  glazed 5, 6, *14–15*, *28–29*, *39*, *42–47*
  rims 41, *42–43*
  unglazed *10*
breakfast sets 24, *26*, *34*
British studio potter movement 21
Britton, Alison 41

Button Factory 16–20
buttons 16, *17–19*, 20, 41

C
'cabbage days' period 30
Camberwell College of Arts 40
ceramic buttons *see* buttons
coffee pots *26*
collectors 49
colour palette 6, 24, 40–41
  see also glazes, coloured glazes; mixed clay designs; terracotta pottery
competitions 11
Coper, Hans 21–23, *22*, 32, 35, 41
critical reception of works 11, 21, 35, 41, 49

D
Dartington Hall 21
designer store customers 30
  see also fashion house customers

E
earthenware 4, *5*, *8–9*, *10*
Eisenstadt 3, 12
exhibitions and displays 4, 11, 32, 35, 49

F
fashion house customers 20
  see also designer store customers
Festival of Britain 32

Flavin, Dan 49
Freud, Ernst 12

G
'Gesamtkunstwerk' concept 13
glazes
  blistered glaze *38*
  for buttons 16, 20
  coloured glazes *cover, 6*, 24, *25–29*, 30, *34*, *37*, 41, *42–43*, *47*
  frothing glaze 35
  layered *8*
  pitted designs 6, *14–15*, *39*, 40
  simulating textiles 32, 41, *44–45*
  see also raw-glazing; sgraffito technique
Gomperz, Benjamin (father) 4, 11

H
Heal's 30
Hoffmann, Josef 4–6, 11
Hyde Park *see* 18 Albion Mews

I
iconic status and works 1, 2
Issey Miyake meets Lucie Rie 49

J
Japan, exhibitions 49
jewellery 16, *27*

K
kilns 11, 20, *22*, 24, 30–32
'knitted' pots 41, *44–45*
Kunstgewerbeschule 4

L
Lampl, Fritz 12–13, 16
Leach, Bernard
  friendship 21, 40
  retail introductions 30
  views of Rie's work 21, 35
Liberty 30

Lobmeyr gallery 11
Lucie Rie: A retrospective exhibition of earthenware, stoneware and porcelain 1926-67 35

M
manganese oxide
  glaze 24, *25–29*, *34*, *37*, *47*
  inlays and rims *28*, *34*, 41, *42–43*, *44–45*
medals and prizes 11, 32
Milan Triennale 32
mixed clay designs 35, 36
Miyake, Issey 41–49
modernist style 1, 6, *9*, 30
Murray, William Staite 21

N
Nazi Austria 2, 12

O
Ohly, William 16, 23
over-glazing 41

P
Palais Stoclet display 4–6
Paris International Exhibition 11
pitted designs 6, *14–15*, *39*, 40
planters 33
Plischke, Ernst, furniture 6, 13, *14–15*
porcelain *29*, 30, *37*, *47*
post-war production 23–24
potters marks *25*, 32
Powolny, Michael 4
Primavera Gallery 32
prizes and medals 11, 32

R
raw-glazing 11, 24
refugees 2, 12, 16, 20, 21–23
retrospective exhibitions 35
Rie, Dame Lucie
  early life and education 2–3, 4

marriage and relationships 6, 11, 13, 16
awards and recognition 2, 11
death and legacy 49
aesthetic vision 4, 6, 23
domestic skills 2, 40
family members 3–4, 11
iconic status of works 1
influences 1–2, 3, 24, 30
modernist philosophy 30
personality and style 1, 30, 49
photos of potter *1 (facing)*, *7*, *22*, *48*
pioneer for women in art 2
refugee from Nazi Austria 2, 12
response of art world 11, 21, 35, 41, 49
teaching 40
tribute to Coper 41
TV documentary 1
Rie, Hans 6
Royal College of Art doctorate 2
Royal Mail, vase stamp 40

S

Second World War 2, 11–13, 16, 20
serving bowls *see* bowls
sgraffito technique 24, *25*, *26–27*, *29*, *37*, *47*
South Bank exhibition 32
speckling, stylistic feature 24
stoneware 24, *26*, *28*, *33*, *34*, *36*, *38–39*, *44–45*
studios *see* workshops
stylistic features
  asymmetry 24, *28*
  manganese rims and inlays *28*, *34*, 41, *42–43*, *44–45*
  mixed clay designs 35, *36*
  sgraffito designs 24, *25*, *26–27*, *29*, *37*, *47*
  speckles and pinholes 24, *28*
  see also glazes

T

tableware *see* bowls; breakfast sets; coffee pots; tea sets
tea sets 6, *9*, *10*, 24, *25*, *31*
techniques
  asymmetric pouring lips 24, *28*
  mixed clays 35, 36
  over-glazing 41
  raw-glazing 11, 24
  sgraffito 24, *25*, *26–27*, *29*, *37*, *47*
  throwing *1*, *7*, 20
terracotta pottery *9*, *10*, 37
throwing technique *1*, *7*, 20

U

"Uncle Sandor" 3, 6, 11, 12
unglazed earthenware *9*, *10*
urban pottery style 30–32

V

vases *8*, *31*, 35, *36–38*, *46*, *48*
Vienna
  First World War 3–4
  influences on creativity 1–2
  Rie's workshop 2, 6, *7*
  Second World War 11–12
  turn of 19th century 2, 4
Vienna Secession 4

W

Wedgwood design rejection 32
Weiner Werkstätte 4, 11, 12
Werkbund gallery 11
Wieselthier, Vally 11
Wolf, Alexander, "Uncle Sandor" 3, 6, 11, 12
workshops
  Albion Mews studio 2, 13, *14–15*, *22*, *31*, 32
  equipment 6, 11, 20, 24, 30
  Vienna 2, 6, *7*

Lucie Rie
By Isabella Smith
Second Edition, 2024

First published in the United Kingdom in 2022 by Eiderdown Books
Eiderdownbooks.com

Series conceived and developed by Eiderdown Books
Text © Isabella Smith
Images © The estate of Dame Lucie Rie. All rights reserved.
Additional © see Image credits

The moral right of the author has been asserted.

All rights reserved. No part of this publication may be reproduced, stored in an electronic retrieval system, or transmitted in any form or by any means, electronic, mechanical, photocopying, recording or otherwise, without the prior written consent from the publisher and copyright owners.

Every effort has been made to ensure images are correctly attributed however if any omission or error has been made please notify the publisher for correction in future editions.

A CIP record for this book is available from the British Library.

ISBN: 978-1-9160416-9-1

Edited by Rebeka Cohen
Indexed by Jan Worrall
Series design by Clare Skeats
Typeset by Clare Skeats in Lelo by Katharina Köhler

The Modern Women Artists logotype is set in Hesse Antiqua which was released in 2018 to mark the 100th birthday of Gudrun Zapf von Hesse. The forms of Hesse Antiqua are based on the metal punches that von Hesse created in 1947 while working as a bookbinder at the Bauer Type Foundry in Frankfurt.

Printed and bound by Latitude
Reprographics by ALTA